Hope: Is this life all there is?

Editorial

I remember a contributor to BBC Radio 4's *Thought for the Day* commenting once that all of life is a preparation for death, and that we should be open about that with young people in schools. His point was that this applies whether or not you have a faith or belief in some kind of afterlife. If death is the end, we should be prepared. If it is not, we should be prepared.

Some people bemoan the way in which we distract ourselves from thinking about our mortality – caught up in the tangible, the transient, the temporal. We should open our eyes! One of my favourite Hindu texts, the story of the man in the well from Mahabharata 11:5, portrays the human condition as one where we are surrounded by terrors, ensnared by trials of life, with death looming, and yet we are distracted by sweet honey – the trivial pleasures of our material world. It suggests that, at the very least, we should be thinking carefully about how we use our time – making choices deliberately rather than thoughtlessly.

This book is intended to help in this process of thinking carefully. It focuses on hope – firstly, what hopes people have in *this* life, and then in any possible future life. There is plenty of scope for disagreement as students learn about different religious and non-religious beliefs about life after death, and consider their impact in people's lives. Exploring the meaning of funeral words and music opens up a range of secular and religious beliefs, and using contemporary film illustrates questions arising from near-death experiences.

Death can be a painful subject, requiring care and sensitivity, of course. This book offers thoughtful, sensitive and interactive ways of exploring some essential ideas about life after death, so that students can develop their understanding as well as clarify and refine their own ideas.

Stephen Pett
Editor

> The topic of death and the afterlife can be upsetting for some students. Teachers should be sensitive to students, especially those who have been recently bereaved, and present activities with care.

Contents

Getting started
Eight ways to introduce a unit on life after death

1 Everyone believes: no one believes

Give students these categories:
Everyone believes/ most people believe/ some people believe/ no one believes.

Give them the following statements. In pairs they have to decide which category the statements fit in. Compare answers with another pair and discuss differences.

- Life is short.
- Life is good.
- Everybody dies some day.
- I am going to live for ever!
- We can take nothing with us when we die.
- This life is not all that there is – we carry on after death in some form.
- We only have one life and should make the most of it.
- Our soul is trapped in our body and has to be reborn many times before it can escape and return to God.
- It is better to be living than to be dead.
- Heaven is necessary to balance all the injustice and suffering in this world.
- Ideas of heaven are just comforting stories.
- Judgment Day is coming.

2 Talking to children about life after death

There are many books that can be used to introduce the topic of death, dying and life after death to young children.
- Ask students to consider what kinds of things the books are likely to say, and how they will do it.
- Get hold of a selection of books and distribute to students in small groups.
- Do the books match their expectations in content and presentation?
- As a class, summarise the beliefs expressed in the books about death and life after death.
- How many books express atheistic, agnostic or religious beliefs? Are there any common features to life after death? How is heaven described? How do people get there?

Some titles include:
Nicholas Allan, *Heaven*
Alan Durant, *Always and Forever*
Susan Varley, *Badger's Parting Gift*
Doris Stickney, *Water Bugs and Dragonflies*
Maria Shriver, *What's Heaven?*
Michael Rosen's Sad Book.

3 Questions, questions

There are lots of questions to ask about life after death. As a way of finding out what students know about beliefs, encouraging them to ask questions can help to give a focus for a unit of study.

Ask students to work in groups. Get them to imagine that there is life after death and they can ask questions of a spirit who has been allowed to return to life on earth. What questions do they ask her?

Evaluate these questions. Are they important? Why/why not? Each group should identify their two most important ones to feed back to the class. The whole class can then identify the most important question (or two) to ask. Why is this so important? Is it because it is fascinating? Unanswerable? Or has some impact on how we should live now?

Compare the questions the class have raised with those in Steve Turner's poem 'Heaven'. Does he have more important or interesting questions? How seriously does he take the idea of heaven? www.rejesus.co.uk/site/module/steve_turners_poems/P10/

4 Question web

Encourage older students to take on some of the big philosophical questions before exploring what religions and beliefs have to say. Give them these questions to chew over in pairs and then fours. Get them to use a large sheet of paper to draw a web of questions and answers: each question provokes two answers (agreeing and disagreeing), which in turn provoke more questions, and more answers, and so on.

If there's a heaven...
- What part of you makes you *you* – body, mind, personality? Which part can you do without in an afterlife and still be you?
- Will you have a physical body? If so, what age are you? Will you stay that age for ever? What if you were disabled in life? If you have a new, recreated body, is it still you or just a replica? How do you know?
- Will you be a disembodied 'soul'? How will you interact with others? How can you recognise and be recognised? What will you *do*?
- What does it mean to live for ever? What is the difference between living in a timeless eternity and everlasting eternity?
- If heaven is all in your mind, does it exist?

5 'Threshold to the Kingdom'

Mark Wallinger's 11-minute video installation shows the arrivals hall at a UK airport. Passengers spill through the doors, alone or with others, ambling or striding purposefully, displaying varying emotions, some greeting waiting relatives, all watched by a bored guard. Played in slow motion to the sound of Allegri's *Miserere*, a setting of Psalm 51, it is, in Wallinger's words, 'a bit slippery … a paradox … ambiguous'. Is this the entrance to heaven?

- Ask students to look at images of the installation (an online image search provides a few) and ask them what they think is going on.
- Give them the title – what difference does this make to their ideas?
- Play Allegri's *Miserere* and read Psalm 51. How does this affect their understanding of the installation?
- Ask students to imagine they are the security guard deciding who shall pass (into heaven?) and who shall be turned away. They should decide the criteria they would use and reflect on how they would feel at having this power.
- How far does the installation reflect Christian belief?

A short (unofficial) clip is available at
http://vimeo.com/18551262

6 Recording good and bad deeds

Recording angels are mentioned in Jewish, Christian and Islamic traditions. In Islam they are known as Kiramin Katibin – noble writers – and two are appointed for each person. Observing from a person's right and left, their role is to record good and bad deeds, to be revealed at Judgment Day.

Hindus, Buddhists and Sikhs also maintain that actions and attitudes are recorded through the law of karma.

The implications are that current actions have an impact on a person's future destiny after death.

- Give students a character from a TV soap opera and get them to watch an episode, acting as recording angels.
- Talk about their findings. Is it easy to decide good and bad deeds? What about intentions? How can they weigh up the value of actions? Do good actions outweigh bad, or the other way around? What consequences should there be for these deeds? How might future happiness or suffering balance current behaviour?

Use this discussion to talk about the moral implications of belief in an afterlife. If there is some kind of heaven, should everyone get in?

7 Vanitas vanitatem

'Vanity of vanities! All is vanity! Life is short, wearisome and meaningless; there is nothing new under the sun.' Thus spoke Ecclesiastes, the wise preacher in the Bible. His words provoked a genre of 'Vanitas art', particularly in seventeenth-century Netherlands, to remind people that life is short.

Do an online image search for some examples of Vanitas art. See if students can work out the symbolism before you give the list below.

Vanitas art usually contains symbols representing:
- arts and sciences (maps, musical instruments)
- earthly pleasures (wine glasses, playing cards)
- wealth and power (jewellery, gold)
- the brevity of life (skulls, fading flowers, smoke)
- resurrection and eternal life (ivy, ears of corn).

Talk about why these were popular (think about the Christian context) and compare with some contemporary examples, such as Damien Hirst's 'For the Love of God' and 'A Thousand Years'.
http://www.damienhirst.com/

Information here: http://bit.ly/19WPjXt

To what extent could Si Smith's cover art be seen as Vanitas art?

8 Five ways to use the cover art

A copiable version of the cover is on the back, and downloadable from the subscribers'/members area of the website.

Ask students:

a Before looking at the artwork, sketch or describe what they would include to match the title: 'Hope: Is this life all there is?'

b What images are missing? Create the six images to fill in the gaps.

c Write a caption for each picture, explaining what it has to do with hope and with life after death.

d Copy the cover art and cut up the individual images. Place the images on a continuum: do they suggest yes, life after death – no life after death?

e Add a *y*-axis to the continuum and put a second continuum from positive to negative. Is the view of life after death expressed in each image positive or negative? Adjust their placements from activity (d).

Hopes for the world: where do you start?

Overview

This unit gives students an opportunity to open up some of the ideas around the concept of hope in this world. Students will have the opportunity to interpret a substantial text from the Jewish scripture/Christian Old Testament writings of the prophet Isaiah. They can show understanding creatively as they think about how young people today might take the vision and apply it to their own community. They explore how some remarkable people set examples as beacons of hope in difficult circumstances.

The guided visualisation strategy gives students a chance to imagine their community, how it can be improved and how with hope they can be part of that improvement process.

Essential knowledge

For religions there are two types of hope: hope for life on earth and hope for what lies beyond. This unit focuses on earthly hopes and perhaps focuses our minds on the slogan the charity Christian Aid used a few years ago: 'we believe in life before death'.

In Islam, hope rests in Allah's mercy, submitting willingly to his rule in a Muslim's life. This also brings with it a responsibility for those around, of course, as in the passionate concern for others shown by Malala Yousafzai and many other Muslims who work to bring justice.

In Buddhism, ideas of impermanence (*anicca* (Pali); *anitya* (Sanskrit)) and loving kindness for all sentient beings (*metta* (Pali); *maitri* (Sanskrit)), are both central to the idea of hope. There is not a sense of some future life to be grasped, but impermanence means that everything changes, even bad situations. This can bring hope. Loving kindness includes the cultivated impulse to bring change for the better for others. Both ideas are exemplified in the practice of engaged Buddhism, and also the work of Daisaku Ikeda.

Essential teaching and learning

This unit supports students in the development of their skills of interpretation, enquiry and reflection. Engaging with texts from key sources is a first-hand engagement, enriched by the example of people whose lives are testimony to their beliefs in hope in this world. In RE, the challenge of right living is often raised, and here students have an opportunity to reflect on their own attitudes and actions.

11–14

Context

These activities would fit into a series of lessons on justice or life after death as well as the study of Christianity, Islam or Buddhism. The idea of hopes for this world links with the key themes of beliefs and ways of living, and to questions of meaning, purpose, values and commitments.

Resources/ links

These links give some background information about the people of hope on p.7.

The UN speech of Malala Yousafzai: www.bbc.co.uk/news/world-asia-23282662

Daisaku Ikeda: www.daisakuikeda.org

A 20-minute clip on the work of Gandhi, Martin Luther King and Ikeda on peace. www.youtube.com/watch?v=l9VexOP9PDg

Nelson Mandela's 1994 Easter speech: http://tinyurl.com/ppxmu6x

Mandela's speeches are available on http://db.nelsonmandela.org/speeches

An REOnline Banquet resource by Mary Myatt explores the work of Gandhi, Martin Luther King and Ikeda on peace. http://tinyurl.com/o2zl5oe

Buddhist meditation gives hope to life-inmates in US prison. Trailer and more information at www.dhammabrothers.com

Learning activities

1 Hopeless world: hopeful world

Show the students a selection of newspaper headlines and articles or watch a news bulletin. Ask the students to list the things that: make them **angry** about the world we live in, make them anxious, frustrated or even **despairing**, or give them **hope** for a better world in the future.

Sort the headlines/articles into three categories: Anger, Despair and Hope. Which of these are helpful feelings? From what they know, what might different religions and beliefs say about each of these feelings?

Create a 'wall of hope' in your classroom. Split the wall into three. Ask the students to record: a little hope – something that might happen today; a middle-sized hope – something that might take a long time for them to reach; a great big hope – something that feels nearly impossible at the moment.

Share with the students that many religious people have two types of hope: hope for this world and for the world beyond life.

2 Using the context

As you read the passage from Isaiah on p.6 to students, get them to draw on paper their interpretation of the place you are reading about, the place of the prophet's vision. Read slowly, with pauses for students to keep up, but don't let it drag. You might have some background music on.

Using p.6 as a resource, students should work in pairs to create a 50-word description of the community that Isaiah was writing for. What must the world have been like to need that vision of the future?

Talk about how that community compares to the community students live in today. Is the vision still appealing today?

Use the activities on p.6 to draw more from the text by getting students to re-present it in a contemporary setting.

3 People of hope

Give groups of students one of the people of hope from p.7. Get them to find three things that these people of hope think is important to do to make the world better. Share and talk about these ideas. Find out a bit more about each person.

Ask students to look at the case studies on p.8. What problems do these young people face that might rob them of their hope?

In groups, ask students to decide who would be most likely to inspire these young people, choosing from p.7. Look up the information about the charities on p.8 and suggest how they might offer some hope for this life.

4 Guided visualisation

The guided visualisation on p.9 gives an opportunity for students to reflect on the ideas of hope and vision in religion and the realities of their own lives and communities. The visualisation asks students to be hopeful, to believe that things can be changed and that they can change things.

If this is a new strategy for students, explain that as they close their eyes or look at the floor you are going to read them a story which you want them to imagine in their minds. Start by using the stilling exercise at the beginning of the visualisation. Once the students are still and relaxed, read the guided story slowly, pausing as appropriate.

In follow-up questions ask the students: How did you feel as you left school? Did your feelings change as you approached your house? What would a perfect town or city be like?

Ask students to write a poem expressing their ideas for a perfect city. Provide a copy of the Isaiah 65 passage to stimulate their writing.

[The LORD says:]

'Behold, I will create
new heavens and a new earth.
The sound of weeping and of crying
will be heard in it no more.
Never again will there be in it
an infant who only lives for a few days,
or an old man who does not live out his years;
he who dies at a hundred
will be thought a mere youth;
he who fails to reach a hundred
will be considered cursed.
They will build houses and dwell in them;
they will plant vineyards and eat their fruit.
No longer will they build houses
and others live in them,
or plant and others eat ...
Every person will sit under their own vine
and under their own fig tree,
and no one will make them afraid,
for the LORD Almighty has spoken ...
For as the days of a tree,
so will be the days of my people;
my chosen ones will long enjoy
the works of their hands.
They will not work hard for nothing
or bear children doomed to misfortune;
for they will be a people blessed by the LORD,
they and their descendants with them.
Before they call I will answer;
while they are still speaking I will hear.
The wolf and the lamb will feed together,
and the lion will eat straw like the ox,
but dust will be the serpent's food.
They will neither harm nor destroy
on all my holy mountain,'
says the LORD.

Isaiah ch.65 vs17a, 19b-25;
Micah ch.4 vs4, adapted from NIV

Task 1
Re-read this passage from Isaiah and Micah with a partner.
Look at the picture you created while your teacher first read out this passage.
What must life have been like for the people this passage was written for? If they needed this vision to give them hope, what was going on? Write a 50-word description of the community that this passage was written for.

Task 2
What are the similarities between this community and the headlines of Anger/Despair/Hope from today's newpapers?
What is the same or different about this world 3000 years ago and the world we live in now? With a partner, come up with a detailed description of the similarities and differences between the two times.

Task 3
Imagine that some Christian teenagers are inspired by this passage. They want to get their church to organise a week of social action in their community. How would they use this passage to persuade the church? How will they inspire them to turn hope and vision into action in the local community?
You could create a poem or a rap or series of freeze-frames to show while the passage is read out. Use your imagination! Get the vision!

Task 4
Think of your local community. What is your hope for the future? Use this skeleton vision to get you started:
    Behold ...
    The sound of ...
    Never again will ...
    They who ...
    They will ...
    No longer ...
    Every person ...
    They will not ...
    This will happen if ...

Malala Yousafzai: Muslim

Malala, born in 1997 in Northern Pakistan, became known as a blog writer in her teens, protesting about the lack of rights to education for girls. In October 2012 she was shot by the Taliban on her way home on the school bus. She nearly died. She has since continued to campaign actively for the rights of girls and women.

> So here I stand... one girl among many. I speak – not for myself, but for all girls and boys. I raise up my voice – not so that I can shout, but so that those without a voice can be heard. Those who have fought for their rights: Their right to live in peace. Their right to be treated with dignity. Their right to equality of opportunity. Their right to be educated.
>
> Dear Friends, on the 9th of October 2012, the Taliban shot me on the left side of my forehead. They shot my friends too. They thought that the bullets would silence us. But they failed. And then, out of that silence came thousands of voices. The terrorists thought that they would change our aims and stop our ambitions but nothing changed in my life except this: weakness, fear and hopelessness died. Strength, power and courage was born. I am the same Malala. My ambitions are the same. My hopes are the same. My dreams are the same.
>
> I do not even hate the Talib who shot me. Even if there is a gun in my hand and he stands in front of me, I would not shoot him. This is the compassion that I have learnt from Muhammad – the prophet of mercy, Jesus Christ and Lord Buddha. This is the legacy of change that I have inherited from Martin Luther King, Nelson Mandela and Muhammad Ali Jinnah. This is the philosophy of non-violence that I have learnt from Gandhi Jee, Bacha Khan and Mother Teresa. And this is the forgiveness that I have learnt from my mother and father. This is what my soul is telling me, be peaceful and love everyone.
>
> from Malala Yousafzai 'Speech to the United Nations', 13 July 2013. Source - BBC News Asia © 2013 BBC

Daisaku Ikeda: Buddhist

Philosopher, peace builder and educator, Daisaku is president of Soka Gakkai, a lay Buddhist organisation for peace. In his teens in the Second World War he witnessed terrible suffering. He has spent his life encouraging dialogue for peace.

- 'No matter how hopeless or bleak things appear, the moment always comes when suddenly our spirit revives, and hope is reborn. That is why we must never give up.'
- 'Our life force, our fundamental energy, is fueled by hope.'
- 'When we possess the treasure of hope, it gives rise to other treasures, too. Hope draws forth our inner potential and strength. Hope is a magic weapon that enables us to make our dreams come true.'
- 'Effort and hard work construct the bridge that connects your dreams to reality. Those who make steady efforts are full of hope. And hope, in turn, arises from steady efforts. Embrace your dreams and advance as far as they can take you.'

Quotations sourced at http://www.ikedaquotes.org/hope/hope834

Nelson Mandela: Christian

For 20 years, Nelson Mandela was imprisoned for attempting to gain racial equality in South Africa. After his release in 1990, he went on to negotiate equal rights for black people and become president of the country that had once imprisoned him. Brought up as a Methodist Christian, he rarely spoke about his faith, so that some claim he was an atheist. But some of his words indicate a faith underlying his actions. Speaking of his experience of Christianity when growing up, he wrote:

> The Church was as concerned with this world as the next: I saw that virtually all of the achievements of Africans seemed to have come about through the missionary work of the Church.
>
> *A Long Walk to Freedom* (Little Brown)
>
> During my lifetime I have dedicated myself to this struggle of the African people. I have fought against white domination, and I have fought against black domination. I have cherished the ideal of a democratic and free society in which all persons live together in harmony and with equal opportunities. It is an ideal which I hope to live for and to achieve. But if needs be, it is an ideal for which I am prepared to die.
>
> Statement from the Rivonia trial 1964: http://tinyurl.com/qcnzcyg
>
> Each Easter marks the rebirth of our faith. It marks the victory of our risen Saviour over the torture of the cross and the grave. Our Messiah, who came to us in the form of a mortal man, but who by his suffering and crucifixion attained immortality. … Our Messiah, whose life bears testimony to the truth that there is no shame in poverty: those who should be ashamed are they who impoverish others, whose life testifies to the truth that there is no shame in being persecuted. Those who should be shamed are they who persecute others.
>
> from Nelson Mandela's 1994 Easter speech,
> from the South African History Online website: http://tinyurl.com/ppxmu6x

Where to go for hope?

Here are four short descriptions of young people in the UK, and four charities that are concerned with the wellbeing of young people. Where might these young people find hope?

Becky (11) and Sean (9) have just been rejected by their third foster family. They were taken away from their parents five years ago because their parents were struggling to cope with looking after them properly. This experience has meant that Becky and Sean are struggling to connect well with the adults who are trying hard to care for them. Becky and Sean are frightened of being rejected. It is hard to trust people.

Tina is 12 and her mum works as a carer. Her dad used to hit her mum and Tina wanted her to get away from her dad. But Tina's mum was worried about how she would pay the bills – food, rent, gas and electricity, council tax, etc. Eventually she left her partner but has ended up getting a pay-day loan to cover her bills. Every week it seems to Tina that her mum is getting crushed by the pressure of trying to earn enough to live *and* pay the debts. The pile of unopened bills grows every month. Tina can't stop thinking about it.

Maryam is 16 and has moved schools from an inner city to a rural academy. There are a few other Muslim pupils there, but as the new girl joining in exam year, she seems to have been noticed. Most girls wore the hijab at her last school but here she is the only one. Some students have made fun of her and she has heard some nasty comments as she goes through the school. She's not used to this! Why can't people just accept her?

Sue is 13. She feels completely rubbish. She gets on with her work but never really seems to make much progress – at least, no one ever says she has done well. She is bullied a bit at school but mostly people seem to ignore her. She wonders why she doesn't have any real friends. She feels worthless.

Christians Against Poverty UK offer support to people struggling with debt, by helping them to organise their finances better.
https://capuk.org/

Luton Churches Education Trust support young people in difficult circumstances, whether in care, or having issues with anger, self-worth, or self-harm, for example.
www.lcet.org/

www.ulfaharts.co.uk encourage young people to develop their creativity, raising educational attainment, improving health, bringing together communities, developing interfaith dialogue and social enterprise. They help young people to find confidence and a way of expressing their identity as individuals and as part of a community.

The London Buddhist Centre is one of many Buddhist groups who offer mindfulness meditation for developing awareness and peace of mind. 'Breathing space' uses mindfulness approaches to help people deal with stress and anxiety. **www.lbc.org.uk/**

Hope for the world: guided visualisation

Script

I want you to take a few moments to relax and be still, then join in a guided story with me. You can opt out if you want to, and just sit quietly, but please don't disturb others in the group who are thinking deeply. [Pause]

Begin by finding a comfortable position – two feet on the floor, straight back, hands resting in your lap or folded together. Close your eyes, and be still, so that your imagination can work. Spend a bit of time noticing your breathing – you might count your breaths, in and out, for a minute or so. See how calm this can make you. [Pause]

Imagine that it is the end of the school day … you are getting ready to go … today you're going to walk home on your own … you know your way … nothing unusual … just picture yourself leaving school at the end of the day … you leave the school … and walk off without looking back … [Pause]

You notice … litter around the school gate has all blown away … or been cleared away … rubbish on the grass … old cans … bags … papers … all gone … instead there are flowers you never noticed before … Everything seems pretty normal … but then you feel something unusual … as if the sun is a bit brighter than usual … the breeze softer … you look around but you can't quite see what is different …

You walk on … there is definitely something different … every little thing seems fresher … brighter … better than usual … your shoes are suddenly comfy …

You stop because you see a rare sight … a rabbit on the grassy land you're passing … it sits there … unafraid … nibbling grass … you watch for a moment or two … and you notice more rabbits in the grass … near the hedge … they're not scared … they don't run off … [Pause]

You go on walking home … and your heart is rather full of happiness and hope … because in some strange way the walk seems different today … the whole place seems cleaned up … at its very best … there's no sign of any vandalism … no one fighting … no name-calling from the others around you. You see an old lady sitting with a small boy … they are chatting together. You realise that your whole town has been changed … made perfect … full of hope … joy … and as you get closer to home you feel excited … will home be different too? … what are your hopes for a home where all your hopes are realised … relationships all positive … no one unwell …?

Now imagine yourself walking towards your home … it looks good … you can see the door … you feel as if you can imagine what might be different when you get home … what will it be like if everything has been made new … perfect … full of hope. [Pause]

In a minute we're going to stop this imaginary story … I wonder what the most hopeful thing you imagined was … what would you imagine for your school … your town … your perfect home? [Pause]

When you have identified the hopes you saw fulfilled … then get ready to open your eyes … remember what the classroom was like before you closed your eyes … remember the people … picture it all in your mind's eye … then when you are ready … open your eyes … be still … be calm.

What do people believe about life after death?

Overview

This unit provides students with opportunities to explore the concept of life after death. It focuses on Christian, Hindu and Muslim perspectives in particular. Students will develop their understanding of what belief in life after death means from these three viewpoints and will express their views with increasing clarity through the work. They will consider how these beliefs about life after death are similar and different, and be given opportunity to express their own response to the idea of life after death.

Essential knowledge

Students need to be able to identify the key beliefs of Christians, Hindus and Muslims about the concept of life after death. They also need to know that there is a real diversity within and between faith traditions, with disagreement over the nature and reality of life after death, just as there is with atheist and agnostic perspectives. A lot can be learned from contrasting different perspectives. Are heaven and hell physical or spiritual concepts? Are resurrection and reincarnation mutually exclusive? Is it the soul or atman, or the physical body that survives death? Why do many people, including those with non-religious beliefs, believe in an afterlife?

From this work, students will learn more about who believes what, and reflect on why. Students will need to be able to recognise and use key terminology such as resurrection, heaven, hell, eternal, soul, hope, purgatory, judgement, reincarnation, karma, samsara, moksha, atman, akhirah, niyyah, dunya, jannah, jahannam, and so on.

Essential teaching and learning

This unit supports students in the development of their skills of interpretation, analysis and evaluation.

It is important to enable students to see that not all members of a religion or belief hold exactly the same beliefs; likewise there are differences between religions and beliefs. Understandings of sacred texts and other sources of authority vary, as do the values and attitudes that are based on those beliefs. The stimulus materials in this unit make these similarities and differences explicit and open them up for discussion and deepening understanding.

11–14

Context

This unit fits with key themes of beliefs and teachings, and questions of meaning, purpose, value and commitment. It would contribute to school units on questions of life after death. It will also fit well with a systematic study of Christianity, Hinduism or Islam.

Resources/ links

Listening to Young People Talking
This is an interactive and fully moderated online collection of comments from 5–19s on a range of religious and spiritual

questions, including thoughts on life after death.
www.natre.org.uk/db

Christianity
This website aims to explain and explore what Christians of all kinds believe.
www.christianity.org.uk

RE:Quest
A website for 4–16s and teachers to support teaching about Christianity.
http://request.org.uk

Kauai's Hindu monastery
An explanation of karma and reincarnation in one Hindu tradition.
www.himalayanacademy.com/readlearn/basics/karma-reincarnation

Plain Islam
This website aims to provide information on Islam and Muslims to non-specialist audiences in a way that is clear, simple and accessible.
www.plainislam.com

The Religion of Islam
A detailed outline of Muslim teaching on death, judgement and life after death.
www.islamreligion.com/articles/38

Learning activities

Activity 1 What do students think religious people believe?

Put pupils in pairs and ask each pair to identify what they *think* Christians, Hindus and Muslims believe about life after death.

Combine each pair with another pair and ask them to agree a group opinion for each of the religions and three questions to which they need answers in order to feel confident in their opinion. Encourage clarification of key terms and identification of their sources of information.

Each group chooses one person to be an 'envoy'. The envoy moves to a new group and tries to get answers to their group's questions. They return to their original group and report back.

Activity 2 What do some young people believe?

Put students in small groups and give them a set of the 15 responses from young people on p.12, cut up and ready to sort. Ask students to sort the statements in a variety of ways, e.g. belief in heaven/hell; belief in reincarnation; reasons for beliefs about life after death; concept of judgement. Note that young people do not always express orthodox beliefs. Note also that the labels given are the young people's own descriptions from the NATRE database (see Resources, p.10).

You might vary this activity by giving students the statements without attribution and ask them to sort them into Christian, Muslim, Hindu, atheist and agnostic. They can then compare with p.12 (and later with more orthodox religious teachings from pp.13-15 – see Activity 3 below).

After each 'sort', ask students to reflect on their findings, commenting on why they think there are differences of opinion between people of the same religion and belief, and between people of different religions and beliefs, and any other observations. Encourage accurate use of key vocabulary and reasons for responses.

How far do the responses answer any of their questions from Activity 1? If more questions are raised, what are they and why? Which response is closest to, and which one furthest away from students' own views on life after death?

Activity 3 What do religions actually teach?

Put students in small groups and give them a copy of pp.13–15, which express some key beliefs from Christianity, Hinduism and Islam on life after death.

Ask students to comment on:

- the **sources** given (What are they? What authority do they have and for whom?)

- the **language** used (What is literal and what is symbol and metaphor? Which is most effective? Why?)

- **differences** of opinion (Why are there differences between people of the same – and different – religions and beliefs?)

- **reasons** for belief (Why do so many people believe there is some form of life after death? What impact would their belief have on their values and attitudes?).

Activity 4 What beliefs do you have about life after death?

Ask students to work individually to express their own questions and beliefs about life after death and why they believe this. A short written statement would be sufficient to show understanding but you might want to encourage a more creative form of expression, such as art, poetry or music.

Outcomes

Students can demonstrate achievement at levels 4–6 in these activities if they can say 'yes' to some of these 'I can' statements.

Description of achievement

I can …

Level 4

- use the right words to show my understanding of Christian, Hindu and Muslim beliefs about life after death

- refer to these beliefs in my own responses to the idea of life after death.

Level 5

- explain how Christians and Muslims share some similar ideas about life after death, and recognise some differences

- express my own views about life after death, giving reasons to support my ideas.

Level 6

- give an informed account of what people believe about life after death, interpreting the views of Christians, Muslims and Hindus

- express an insight into why people might believe in life after death or not, showing understanding of a perspective I don't agree with.

This unit helps students in Scotland to achieve RME 3-01a; 3-04a.

Life after death: what do young people say?

1
I think that when you die there are two parts of you – the body and the soul. The body lies in the grave but the soul goes on to something else. I am not sure what, whether you are re-incarnated or go on to some afterlife, be it good or bad, but I don't think that death is the end.

Girl, 14, no belief

2
This all fits together because we start off as something like a plant and keep getting reincarnated. Our atman stays the same, though, and after a long time, if you do good, you will reach moksha.

Boy, 13, Hindu

3
I believe in an after life but sometimes I am afraid of death. I think when people die they live in another world. I think the criminals are still accepted by God because God will forgive everyone if you want to be forgiven.

Girl, 11, Christian

4
I think that when we die, our bodies will be blessed and our sins forgiven but I think there is no life after death – we just lie there forgiven and sinless.

Boy, 13, Humanist

5
I believe that when you die you're taken to heaven and given the choice of what you want to go back as, e.g. woman, animal, man or even to start again which is why sometimes you see somebody nearly the same as you.

Girl, 14, no belief

6
I believe that when you die you either go to heaven or hell according to how you've treated others. If you've been bad to others and caused them great pain then you go to hell. If you've been kind to others then God will look after you in heaven.

Girl, 14, Christian

7
When someone dies their soul leaves their body and two angels are sent by Allah question it. If you are a good Muslim you will go to jannah (heaven), however if you have been a bad Muslim you will be punished, but eventually there will be a day where Allah will forgive you.

Boy, 14, Muslim

8
It is so blatant that nobody knows what happens when we die. One half of me believes that life should be taken at face value and expect no reward – when you die, you're dead. Although the other half of me does not believe in the traditional ideas of heaven and hell, I like to think that there is something after death.

Girl, 15, Humanist

9
I think that there must be life after death, because there must be a purpose to our life after life on this earth. I believe that heaven will be a paradise which has no walls and the amount of people who enter is endless. However it will be only a privilege to people who have only done good during their life on this earth.

Boy, 13, Hindu

10
I think that no one really dies. I think that everyone goes to a peaceful place where they reunite with the people who they loved and who passed away before them.

Girl, age 13, Atheist

11
After death, electrical activity stops in the brain. This electrical activity is, in essence, us. I believe that there is nothing after death, as there is nothing to support our consciousness.

Boy, 14, Atheist

12
I believe in heaven and hell and I also believe in an afterlife, and leaving a place you know to go to a place you don't know. I believe that you become an angel when you die and would meet your family that have died.

Girl, 11, no belief

13
I think that there is some kind of life after death because what's the point of us living for 100 years and then leaving? I think death is to balance out the world so it doesn't get crowded and then when we die we go to a different bigger place; it's just like moving house.

Boy, 13, no belief

14
I believe that when I die I will rise again when Jesus returns, but I also believe that Jesus could return tomorrow. If Jesus returns tomorrow he will judge both the living and the dead.

Boy, 12, Christian

15
I am a Muslim and I know that I will be punished for all the sins I have committed. However, I will be rewarded for following the right path. I know I will enter heaven at the end because all Muslims do.

Girl, 15, Muslim

C1

59. L'Ascension - Ascension (Lc 24,50)

© Vie de Jésus Mafa 24, rue du Maréchal Joffre - 78000 Versailles France - www.jesusmafa.com

C2

Jesus said: 'My Father wants everyone who sees the Son to have faith in him and to have eternal life. Then I will raise them to life on the last day.'

Bible, John 6:40 (CEV)

C4

Jesus said: 'I am the resurrection and the life – no one comes to the Father except through me.'

Bible, John 11:25 (CEV)

C3

The Apostle Paul said: 'If we preach that Christ was raised from death how can some of you say that the dead will not be raised to life? If they won't be raised to life, Christ himself wasn't raised to life. And if Christ wasn't raised to life, our message is worthless, and so is your faith. If the dead won't be raised to life, we have told lies about God by saying that he raised Christ to life when he really did not. … But Christ has been raised to life!'

Bible, 1 Corinthians, 15:12-20 (CEV)

C5

The Apostle Paul said: 'Some of you have asked, "How will the dead be raised to life? What kind of bodies will they have?" Don't be foolish. A seed must die before it can sprout from the ground. Wheat seeds and all other seeds look different from the sprouts that come up. … That's how it will be when our bodies are raised to life. These bodies will die, but the bodies that are raised will live for ever. These ugly and weak bodies will become beautiful and strong. As there are physical bodies, there are spiritual bodies. And our physical bodies will be changed into spiritual bodies.

Bible, 1 Corinthians 15:35-44 (CEV)

C6

There is a belief among some Roman Catholic and Orthodox Christians that there is a transitional state between this life and heaven known as Purgatory. This is a place where human souls can be purified and made ready to spend eternity with God. It is seen as joyless, because justice needs to be done for a lifetime's wrongdoing, but it can be shortened by the prayers of those still alive on earth.

www.christianity.org.uk

C7 A Christian perspective

'As a Christian, I believe that death is the end for my physical body, but that my **soul**, which is **eternal**, lives on. My belief in the **resurrection** of Jesus is what gives me **hope** that there is **life after death**. It also means that I believe that at some point I will be given a **new, resurrected body**, like Jesus.

'What happens to me after death will depend on how I have lived my life. If I believe that **Jesus rose from the dead**, trust that Jesus will **forgive** my sins if I ask, and try to follow Jesus' teachings as much as I can, then I will spend eternity in the presence of God, in **heaven**. Some of my friends believe heaven is not a physical place, but if we have bodies like Jesus, we need somewhere to live! The Bible talks about a new heaven and a new earth.

'Some people also think of **hell** as a **physical** place, but I prefer to think of it as a **spiritual** state of eternal **separation** from God. Some Christians believe that there is no hell at all, because God, who is a God of love, accepts everyone regardless of what they have done.'

C8

Jesus said: 'When the Son of Man comes in his glory with all his angels, he will sit on his royal throne. The people of all nations will be brought before him, and he will separate them as shepherds separate their sheep from their goats.

'He will place the sheep on his right and the goats on his left. Then the king will say to those on his right, "My Father has blessed you! Come and receive the kingdom that was prepared for you before the world was created." … Then the king will say to those on his left, "Get away from me! You are under God's curse. Go into the everlasting fire prepared for the devil and his angels."'

Then Jesus said, 'Those people will be punished for ever. But the ones who pleased God will have eternal life.'

Bible, Matthew 25:31-46 (CEV)

Hinduism: life after death

H1

Reincarnation © Himalayan Academy Publications, Kapaa, Kauai, Hawaii. Used under the Creative Commons licence.

H2

Just as a person casts off worn-out garments and puts on others that are new, even so does the embodied soul cast off worn-out bodies and take on others that are new.

Bhagavad Gita, 2.26

H4

As a caterpillar, having reached the end of a blade of grass, takes hold of another blade and draws itself to it, so the Self (atman), having left behind a body unconscious, takes hold of another body and draws it to himself.

Brihadaranyaka Upanishad 4.3.34f

H3

As a goldsmith, taking an old ornament, moulds it into another, newer and more beautiful, so the Self (atman), having given up the body and left it unconscious, takes on a new and better form, either that of the Fathers, or that of the Celestial Singers, or that of the gods, or that of other beings, heavenly and earthly.

Brihadaranyaka Upanishad 4.3.34f

H5

Where people of goodwill and good deeds rejoice, their bodies now made free from all disease, their limbs made whole from lameness or defect. In that heaven may we behold our parents and our sons!

Atharva Veda 6.120.3

H6

A person who is not disturbed by the incessant flow of desires – that enter like rivers into the ocean which is ever being filled but is always still – can alone achieve peace, and not the man who strives to satisfy such desires.

Bhagavad Gita, 2.70

H7

As a person acts, so he becomes in life. Good deeds make one pure; bad deeds make one impure. We are what our desire is. As our desire is, so is our will. As our will is, so are our acts. As we act, so we will become. We live in accordance with our deep, driving desire. It is according as one conducts oneself, so does one become. The doer of good becomes good. The doer of evil becomes evil. One becomes virtuous by virtuous action, bad by bad action.

Brihadaranyaka Upanishad, 4.4.5

H8

The wheel of life moves on …. It is overwhelmed by weakness and grief, and it has diseases and calamities for its children. That wheel relates in time and place. It has toil and exercise for its noise. Day and night are the rotations of that wheel. It is encircled by heat and cold. Pleasure and pain are its joints, and hunger and thirst are the nails fixed into it. Sunshine and shade are the ruts it causes. It is capable of being agitated during even such a short space of time as is taken up by the opening and the closing of the eyelid. It is enveloped in the terrible waters of delusion. It is ever revolving and void of consciousness. It is measured by months and half months. It is not uniform, being ever changing, and moves through all the worlds.

Mahabharata, 45

H9 A Hindu perspective

In Hindu teaching, the ultimate force for life **(Brahman)** is in everything. In the individual this is identified as **atman** (for some Hindus that's the same as Brahman; others see the two as distinct). Atman continues after death when either it achieves **moksha** (liberation) and is absorbed into Brahman or it is re-housed or re-clothed in another body.

This **cycle** of birth, death, rebirth is called **samsara**. It is your **karma** in this life that determines what your **reincarnation** will be. If a person dies in Varanasi (Benares), on the banks of river Ganges, then they will not be reborn. So some Hindus who know they are about to die make a last pilgrimage hoping to die there.

I1

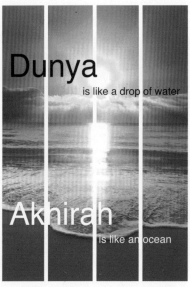

Dunya
is like a drop of water

Akhirah
is like an ocean

© istock/idizimage

I2

It is Allah who gives you life, then gives you death; then he will gather you together for the Day of Judgment.

Qur'an 45.36

I4

Allah has promised to believers, men and women, gardens under which rivers flow, to dwell in. And beautiful mansions in gardens of everlasting bliss. But the greatest bliss is the good pleasure of Allah: that is the supreme felicity.

Qur'an, 9.72

I3

The trumpet will be sounded, when all that are in the heavens and on earth will swoon, except such as it will please Allah to exempt. Then will a second one be sounded, when, behold, they will be standing and looking on!

And the earth will shine with the glory of its Lord. The Record of Deeds will be placed open; the prophets and the witnesses will be brought forward; and just decisions pronounced between them; and they will not be wronged (in the least). And to every soul will be paid in full (the fruit) of its deeds; and Allah knows best all that they do.

Qur'an, 39. 68–70
A detailed description of the Final Judgment is found in: Qur'an, 68. 13 – 33

I6

O thou Creator of the heavens and the earth! Thou art my protector in this world (dunya) and in the hereafter (akhirah).

Qur'an, 12.101

I7

No one in heaven or on the earth knows the Unseen save God; and they know not when they will be raised. Does [human] knowledge extend to the hereafter? No, for they are in doubt concerning it. No, for they cannot see it.

Qur'an, 26.65-66

I5

The Prophet said, 'When a human being is laid in his grave and his companions return and he even hears their footsteps, two angels come to him and make him sit and ask him: "What used you to say about this man, Muhammad?" He will say: "I testify that he is Allah's slave and His Apostle." Then it will be said to him, "Look at your place in the Hell-Fire. Allah has given you a place in Paradise instead of it."'

The Prophet added, 'The dead person will see both these places. But a non-believer or a hypocrite will say to the angels, "I do not know, but I used to say what the people used to say!" It will be said to him, "Neither did you know nor did you take the guidance (by reciting the Quran)."

'Then he will be hit with an iron hammer between his two ears, and he will cry and that cry will be heard by whatever approaches him except human beings and jinns.'

Hadith Sahih Bukhari 2:422

I8 A Muslim perspective

In Islam, the person is Allah's unique creation. We are a physical **body** and a spiritual **soul** with the freedom of choice to live in submission to Allah or not. **Resurrection** of the body and **eternal life** after death **(akhirah)** are part of our fundamental beliefs. Death is a part of the will of Allah, a natural part of life.

We trust in Allah, the merciful, and in His goodness. Belief, actions and intentions **(niyyah)** in this life are important for the outcome of the Day of Judgment **(Yawm ad-Din)**. For the faithful Muslim, paradise **(jannah)** is the reward. Those who reject Allah's path and guidance will finish in hell **(jahannam)**.

Topical film:
Hereafter

Synopsis

The film follows three stories that gradually come together.

Marie Lelay is a French TV journalist, on holiday in Thailand with her lover, Didier. She gets caught up in the 2004 tsunami and is left for dead by rescuers. But after a near-death experience, she wakes up. The experience has a profound effect on her life. Unable to continue with the pressure of being a political interviewer, she pursues her interest in near-death experiences and writes a book: *Hereafter: The Conspiracy of Silence*.

George Lonegan is a factory worker in San Francisco. He is a psychic, seeming to have a genuine ability to make 'connections' with a person's dead relatives through a simple touch, but is reluctant to do so. His brother, Billy, wants him to make the most of his 'gift' – he sees a fortune to be made. But George sees his 'gift' as a curse, destroying the possibility of true relationships for him, as shown in the impact on his promising friendship with evening-class partner, Melanie. George leaves his brother's scheming behind and travels to London.

Marcus and Jason are twin 11-year-old Londoners trying to look after their drug-addict mother in the face of concern from social services. Jason is killed in an accident, leaving Marcus bereft and adrift. His mother goes into rehab and he goes to a foster family. He searches for comfort through a series of psychics, but without success.

The characters all arrive at the London Book Fair for the denouement.

You might use *Hereafter* to explore the following questions:

 Is there life after death?

The film links two phenomena often used in arguments for an afterlife: near-death experiences (NDEs) and psychic communication with the dead. Marie says her book about NDEs is scientific, arising from research into many accounts that are strikingly similar, with widespread evidence of people having NDEs. George makes no such claims for scientific rigour. In fact, the psychics consulted by Marcus are presented as charlatans. Within the film, we believe George has some kind of psychic experience. It seems genuine because of his sympathetic portrayal, but this is not evidence for continuing life, of course. It is easy to give astonishingly accurate details of a person's deceased loved one when it is scripted.

Many argue that death is the end: 'the lights go out … the plug's pulled … the eternal void,' as Didier puts it. NDEs represent the workings of an oxygen-starved brain. Is it because people often long for comfort in the face of loss, that makes NDEs and claimed psychic phenomena persuasive evidence for life after death, or is the evidence compelling in its own right?

 Can near-death experiences reveal the nature of any life hereafter?

In the film, Marie and clinic director Dr Rousseau describe the common characteristics of an NDE. It is peaceful and quiet; there is light and a feeling of weightlessness; there is often a sense of the presence of others. The portrayal of Marie's experience suggests that other people are present as vaguely physical beings, in more or less recognisable forms. Does this suggest that an afterlife is physical or non-physical? In what way could it be interactive with this world?

There does seem to be quite a lot of hanging about in this screen afterlife. The dead seem to be rather more interested in what is going on in the world they have left behind than making the most of the one in which they find themselves. Would that be an ultimately satisfying experience? Does it say more about our current lives than any possible hereafter?

Perhaps for those who have NDEs, the sensation of peace is most powerful, particularly in contrast to the usually traumatic circumstances in which these experiences often occur – such as Marie's shocking tsunami experience. In these cases, philosophical questions about the nature of the afterlife are overwhelmed by the conviction that something good awaits.

How does death affect the living?

Many people want there to be some form of life after death. For some, this is an argument for life after death – this longing represents the eternal within in the temporal, human beings transcending the material realm. Some might argue that justice demands that good and bad deeds are dealt with in some ultimate fashion – one argument for the law of karma, for example. For others, this belief is a form of wish fulfilment, a desire for significance beyond the limits of our human existence, arising out of weakness.

How you interpret experiences will reflect your beliefs. In his book *Faith and Knowledge* John Hick recounts the 'parable of the celestial city', where two travellers go along the same path but experience it differently: the atheist believes there is no destination; the theist believes they are travelling to the 'celestial city'. Both interpret all of their experiences in the light of their beliefs. In a similar way, Marcus sees the loss of his cap in the Charing Cross tube station not as a random (albeit lucky) event but as evidence that Jason is looking after him.

The film does show that, for most people, the death of a loved one is shattering, a cause of much grief and pain. There are several poignant scenes to this effect. The desire for consolation is obvious: where do people look for comfort? Where can it be found?

Does religious belief offer genuine comfort?

Religion does not feature much in the film, and references to it are not positive. The priest at Jason's funeral is lacking in interest and humanity, his words of comfort appear formulaic and are belied by his offhand manner:

> Death is not final, it is merely the beginning, gateway to an afterlife that reflects our conduct here on earth. God in his infinite generosity created heaven, which is where Jason is now, surrounded by all the angels and saints, looking down at us. And so we commit Jason's body to dust, his soul already in God's care.

Religion seems to offer little to Marcus and his mother. The priest, like the psychics, is just one more fraudster.

Clearly, this is not the case for many people of faith around the world and through the centuries. Compare the film's words with the Anglican funeral service, which looks to the mercy of God for consolation:

> Almighty God, you judge us with infinite mercy and justice and love everything you have made. In your mercy turn the darkness of death into the dawn of new life, and the sorrow of parting into the joy of heaven; through our Saviour, Jesus Christ. Amen.

Christians believe life after death is dependent upon God's mercy rather than the dreams and wishes of human beings. But the film still raises the question as to whether such comfort is genuine or illusory. If someone feels comforted, does that matter? Or, as the apostle Paul wrote, is an illusory belief in resurrection to be pitied (1 Corinthians 15:17-18)?

What makes life worth living?

The film reminds us that life is vulnerable to chance and misfortune (like the tsunami) as well as malice (such as the teenagers bullying Jason). However, it also shows clearly that life is full of rich experiences *now*. The food-tasting scene between George and Melanie highlights the vivid and sensual reality of ordinary life. Is it better to think that the connections we have with the living are more important than any with the dead? Is it true that 'a life that's all about death is no life at all'?

Some alternative films

Big Fish (2003): What difference would it make if you knew how and when you are going to die? In this film, Edward Bloom finds out as a child how he is going to die. It makes him very confident when he faces challenges, as he has no fear. It makes him ambitious to seek and find what really matters.

After Life (1998): A Japanese film where, after death, people go into a waiting area. Their task is to recall and recreate a scene from their lives that they will live in for ever – a process which involves resolving and reconciling things that have happened in life.

The Fountain (2006): A rather languid film exploring love, loss, bereavement and the desire for immortality.

What do funerals tell us about life, death and life after death?

Overview

Funerals are the closest most of us get to death. They reveal much about our attitudes to and beliefs about life, death and life after death, not least through the music and readings used.

This unit focuses on Christian and secular worldviews. It explores how the hymns and songs used at funerals show changing beliefs and attitudes. Students compare the words of a popular song with a religious hymn, examining the differences between secular and Christian beliefs and attitudes. Comparing common ideas of heaven with biblical texts is another way of trying to see the difference between popular impressions and the relatively limited information in the Bible. Extension work interprets a reading that is commonly used at funerals.

Essential knowledge

Students should know that even among people with no particular religious faith there is more than a residual belief in some kind of afterlife. Many of the popular songs played at funerals express this idea that life continues in some form, and the dead person has not just ceased to be. The most popular song, 'My Way', expresses a more materialist perspective, however, and many atheists are robust in looking for significance in this life rather than hoping for it in another.

Christian beliefs about heaven stress the dependence of existence upon God. Some Christians believe in the immortality of the soul, which naturally continues after death, to be joined with a resurrected body at some point in the future. Others stress that God recreates a person in an entirely unnatural act. Roman Catholic teaching is that heaven involves the resurrected body reunited with the soul and enjoying the timeless beatific vision of God. The Bible presents the idea of a transformed cosmos, a new heaven and a new earth.

The biblical texts to do with heaven rely upon symbolism from the Jewish Bible/ Christian Old Testament. Hence the talk of a garden (from Eden) and a city (a new Jerusalem) built on twelve foundation stones (the tribes of Israel), with the river of life and the tree of knowledge reflecting a completion of the creation and 'Fall' narratives in Genesis. How these texts are interpreted is complex!

Essential teaching and learning

Getting students to wrestle with original source material is a good way of engaging with beliefs, rather than rely upon summary descriptions. This gives them the opportunity to interpret, analyse and evaluate ideas and beliefs, and to apply their learning. Having an opportunity (on p.23) to see how taking a passage out of context can completely distort what the writer originally intended offers a valuable lesson in RE, when we often use short extracts to illustrate a point without setting the context. Bear that in mind when using p.22!

13–16

Context

This unit raises key questions about meaning and purpose in life. It would fit in a series of lessons on beliefs about life after death, or a study of Christian beliefs, compared with non-religious views. The resources can contribute to examination courses as well as working with 13–14s.

Resources/ links

The Co-operative Funeralcare guide, *The Ways We Say Goodbye*, 2013.
http://bit.ly/1gGy77I

www.funeralhelper.org gives a selection of popular songs and hymns, as well as religious and non-religious readings used at funerals.

More resources are available from www. naturalendings.co.uk

A personal non-religious guide to preparing for a funeral, from Emma Freud in the *Guardian*:
http://bit.ly/19bNYve

Henry Scott Holland's full text for 'The King of Terrors':
http://en.wikisource.org/wiki/The_King_of_Terrors

 Additional strategies for using the Scott Holland text are available to download for subscribers/members.

Interesting and clear summaries of Christian beliefs about life after death from former Anglican Bishop Tom Wright, including interpretations of some of the texts from p.23: http://bit.ly/1gkMk9Q Not all Christians agree with these interpretations, but they do represent a mainstream view.

Learning activities

1 What does our choice of music say about attitudes to life and death?

Use the information from the Co-operative Funeralcare survey on p.20.

a Ask students what music these people might choose for their funeral: an accountant, a farmer, an X Factor judge, a *Marvel* superhero, a Christian youth worker?

b Give out the information: which of these songs/hymns might suit the individuals in the first activity and why?

c Discuss: What do these choices say about the people who have chosen them? What do people look for in their choice of music for funerals? Why are these songs/hymns popular? Does this tell us anything about our society (e.g. values of the wartime generation; an increasingly secular society; hopes of an afterlife)?

d Listen to some of the songs, hymns and music. Ask students what mood the music would give to a funeral service and why.

e Find and print out copies of the words for some of these songs (see Resources p.18). Get students to compare a song and a hymn, and note similarities and differences. What beliefs about life, death and life after death do they reveal? Copy p.21 to support students analysing and interpreting the texts.

f Ask students to rewrite 'My Way' or 'You'll Never Walk Alone' as specifically Christian songs. What would they need to change to express the idea of getting to heaven through Jesus?

2 Making sense of heaven

a Ask small groups of students to describe the features of heaven, from their own ideas, recording them on large sheets of paper.

b Give them a selection of secular songs and readings and get them to add any further ideas they find here, or note where these match their ideas.

c Use some of the most popular biblical readings to illustrate what Christians believe about heaven (some key texts on p.22). What similarities and differences can they see between the ideas they have collected so far and the biblical ideas?

d Do an online search for heaven in art. Students might match the images to one of the biblical sources. To what extent do these images express a popular or biblical view? (www.artbible.info is a good source of biblical images.)

3 Extension activities: interpreting text and context

Henry Scott Holland's 'Death is nothing at all', from a sermon preached soon after the death of Edward VII in 1910, is a popular text at religious and non-religious funerals. Give students the extracts from p.23, one at a time.

a Read Section 1. Talk about what the passage means and why it is such a popular reading. How would you read it aloud? What music would accompany it appropriately? How does it comfort people? Do students agree with its message? Why/why not?

b Section 1 shows one way people might respond to death, Holland says. It does not reflect his own views. The second passage is another way we respond. Ask students to read this. How different is the tone? What music is appropriate for this? Does it reflect a real response to death? Why is this passage not read out at funerals?

c This difficult passage shows the distinctively Christian heart of Holland's talk, which is missing from the popular reading. Work through this with students, clarifying what Holland means. Talk about how knowing the context can change our interpretation. Ask them to write short summaries of the three perspectives in the Holland text, as for a newspaper report on the funeral.

d In the light of their studies in this unit, ask students to respond to the following statement, giving different viewpoints including their own, using evidence and argument: *Funerals are for the living, not the dead.*

Outcomes

Students can demonstrate achievement at levels 4–7 in these activities if they can say 'yes' to some of these 'I can' statements.

Description of achievement

I can …

Level 4

- show that I understand what some non-religious songs and some Christian hymns say about life after death

- create a statement of my own beliefs about life after death, referring to Christian and secular ideas from the songs.

Level 5

- explain the impact of funeral services, and the words used, on Christians and on people without a religious faith

- connect my own beliefs about life after death with a view I disagree with, in the light of learning about funeral services.

Level 6

- interpret religious and non-religious texts used at funerals and explain how they are used to show beliefs about life, death and life after death

- consider the advantages and disadvantages of believing or not believing in life after death for someone attending a funeral, expressing my own insights.

Level 7

- account for some of the ways in which funerals retain a belief in life after death even in a secular country

- express personal and critical evaluations of the idea that funerals are for the living, not the dead.

This unit helps students in Scotland to achieve RME 3-06a, 4-06a.

Funeral songs: what do they tell us about attitudes to life and death?

The Co-operative Funeralcare Survey of 2012* shows some of the current preferences for funerals in the UK. The findings suggest that there is a shift away from mourning to celebration, with less of a focus on death and more on the life of the person who has died. The survey comments: 'What many people are celebrating is the uniqueness of the individual: their character, their passions and interests, the things that made them unique. Increasingly they are arranging funerals to capture these aspects of a person's life.'

Here are the Top 10 hymns, songs and pieces of music from the 2012 survey, along with a selection of more quirky choices of music.

Top 10 Hymns

1 'Abide With Me'
2 'The Lord is my Shepherd'
3 'All Things Bright and Beautiful'
4 'The Old Rugged Cross'
5 'How Great Thou Art'
6 'Amazing Grace'
7 'Jerusalem'
8 'Morning has Broken'
9 'The Day Thou Gavest, Lord, is Ended'
10 'Make Me a Channel of Your Peace'

Top 10 songs

1 'My Way' (Frank Sinatra and others)
2 'Time to Say Goodbye' (Sarah Brightman/Andrea Bocelli)
3 'Wind Beneath My Wings' (Bette Midler)
4 'Over the Rainbow' (Eva Cassidy)
5 'Angels' (Robbie Williams)
6 'You Raise Me Up' (Josh Grobin/Westlife and others)
7 'You'll Never Walk Alone' (Gerry and the Pacemakers)
8 'We'll Meet Again' (Vera Lynn)
9 'My Heart Will Go On' (Celine Dion)
10 'Unforgettable' (Nat King Cole)

Top 10 pieces of classical music

1 'Nimrod', from Enigma Variations (Elgar)
2 Canon in D (Pachelbel)
3 'Ave Maria' (Schubert)
4 'Nessun Dorma' (Puccini)
5 'Pie Jesu' from Requiem (Fauré)
6 The Four Seasons (Vivaldi)
7 'Adagio in G' (Albinoni)
8 'Air', from 3rd Orchestral Suite (Bach)
9 'Largo', from Xerxes (Handel)
10 'Clair de Lune' (Debussy)

A selection of other choices

'Always Look on the Bright Side of Life' (Eric Idle)
'Yin Tong Song' (Spike Milligan)
'Bat out of Hell' (Meatloaf)
'Spirit in the Sky' (Doctor and the Medics)
'Clock Theme', from Countdown
Match of the Day theme
One Foot in the Grave theme
Last of the Summer Wine theme
Six Feet Under theme
'It's Time to Face the Music' (The Muppets theme)

Information

- In 2005, hymns accounted for 55% of music chosen, popular songs 40%, and classical music 5%.
- In 2009, hymns accounted for 41%, and by 2012 this had dropped to 30%, with only 4% requesting a piece of classical music.
- Just over 10% of funerals arranged are 'humanist', led by a humanist officiant or family and friends. 'People don't just want religion spoken about – they want the person spoken about.'
- Around 25% of funeral homes have refused to play a piece of music on the grounds of taste. These include Queen's 'Another One Bites the Dust', and John Lennon's 'Imagine', with the line, 'Imagine there's no heaven'.

*Information found at www.co-operative.coop/Funeralcare/brochures/march2013/The-way-we-say-goodbye/

Interpreting beliefs and attitudes to life and death in two funeral songs

- Select one hymn and one song; listen to the music and read the lyrics.
- What beliefs do they express? For each line in column 1, put a number from 1 to 5 in the other two columns (1 means the song/hymn doesn't show this belief; 5 means this is an important belief in the song/hymn).
- Write down what evidence there is that this song/hymn shows or does not show this view of life and death.
- What other beliefs are expressed? Add them to the grid below.

Belief about life and death	Hymn name	Song name
This life is all there is. I need to take it by the scruff of the neck. Seize the day!		
Death is the end. That is it. No life after death, no heaven, nothing.		
There is something after death – some form of existence.		
There is a God.		
There is a heaven – a place without the fears and suffering of this world.		
God guided and kept me through life and will guide and keep me through death.		
Jesus is the way to heaven.		
Family and friends – they are what matter most in life.		
After death, people stay alive in our memories.		
At death there is some form of judgement about how we have lived our lives.		

Deeper thinking

- Was your hymn/song written to be sung at funerals? How do you know? Why do you think they are popular? How might they bring comfort to family and friends?
- Write your top five pieces of advice for someone choosing music for a funeral. What differences will you need to include if you are writing for an atheist, an agnostic or a Christian?

Life after death: heaven in Christianity

Jesus said: 'Very truly I tell you, whoever hears my word and believes him who sent me has eternal life and will not be judged but has crossed over from death to life. Very truly I tell you, a time is coming and has now come when the dead will hear the voice of the Son of God and those who hear will live. ...

'Do not be amazed at this, for a time is coming when all who are in their graves will hear his voice and come out – those who have done what is good will rise to live, and those who have done what is evil will rise to be condemned.'

John 5:24-25, 28-29 (NIV)

Jesus said: 'Do not let your hearts be troubled. You believe in God; believe also in me. My Father's house has many rooms; if that were not so, would I have told you that I am going there to prepare a place for you? And if I go and prepare a place for you, I will come back and take you to be with me that you also may be where I am. You know the way to the place where I am going.' Thomas said to him, 'Lord, we don't know where you are going, so how can we know the way?' Jesus answered, 'I am the way and the truth and the life. No one comes to the Father except through me. If you really know me, you will know my Father as well.'

John 14:1-7 (NIV)

Listen, I tell you a mystery: We will not all sleep, but we will all be changed – in a flash, in the twinkling of an eye, at the last trumpet. For the trumpet will sound, the dead will be raised imperishable, and we will be changed. For the perishable must clothe itself with the imperishable, and the mortal with immortality. When the perishable has been clothed with the imperishable, and the mortal with immortality, then the saying that is written will come true: 'Death has been swallowed up in victory.'
'Where, O death, is your victory?
   Where, O death, is your sting?'
The sting of death is sin, and the power of sin is the law. But thanks be to God! He gives us the victory through our Lord Jesus Christ.

1 Corinthians 15:51-56 (NIV)

After this I looked, and there before me was a door standing open in heaven. ... there before me was a throne in heaven with someone sitting on it. And the one who sat there had the appearance of jasper and ruby. A rainbow that shone like an emerald encircled the throne. Surrounding the throne were twenty-four other thrones, and seated on them were twenty-four elders. They were dressed in white and had crowns of gold on their heads. ... The twenty-four elders fall down before him who sits on the throne and worship him... and say:
'You are worthy, our Lord and God,
   to receive glory and honour and power,
for you created all things,
   and by your will they were created
   and have their being.'

Revelation 4: 1-4, 10-11 (NIV)

Then I saw 'a new heaven and a new earth,' for the first heaven and the first earth had passed away, and there was no longer any sea. I saw the Holy City, the new Jerusalem, coming down out of heaven from God, prepared as a bride beautifully dressed for her husband. And I heard a loud voice from the throne saying, 'Look! God's dwelling place is now among the people, and he will dwell with them. They will be his people, and God himself will be with them and be their God. "He will wipe every tear from their eyes. There will be no more death" or mourning or crying or pain, for the old order of things has passed away.'

Revelation 21:1-4 (NIV)

Then the angel showed me the river of the water of life, as clear as crystal, flowing from the throne of God and of the Lamb down the middle of the great street of the city. On each side of the river stood the tree of life, bearing twelve crops of fruit, yielding its fruit every month. And the leaves of the tree are for the healing of the nations. No longer will there be any curse. The throne of God and of the Lamb will be in the city, and his servants will serve him. They will see his face, and his name will be on their foreheads. There will be no more night. They will not need the light of a lamp or the light of the sun, for the Lord God will give them light. And they will reign for ever and ever.

Revelation 22:1-5 (NIV)

What is the Christian hope?

These words of Canon Henry Scott Holland, from a sermon given in 1910, are often used in funerals. What does he think about death? What is his hope?

> **1** Death is nothing at all. It does not count. I have only slipped away into the next room. Nothing has happened. Everything remains exactly as it was. I am I, and you are you, and the old life that we lived so fondly together is untouched, unchanged. Whatever we were to each other, that we are still. Call me by the old familiar name.
> Speak of me in the easy way which you always used. Put no difference into your tone. Wear no forced air of solemnity or sorrow. Laugh as we always laughed at the little jokes that we enjoyed together. Play, smile, think of me, pray for me. Let my name be ever the household word that it always was. Let it be spoken without an effort, without the ghost of a shadow upon it.
> Life means all that it ever meant. It is the same as it ever was. There is absolute and unbroken continuity. What is this death but an insignificant accident? Why should I be out of mind because I am out of sight? I am but waiting for you, for an interval, somewhere very near, just round the corner. All is well. Nothing is hurt; nothing is lost. One brief moment and all will be as it was before. How we shall laugh at the trouble of parting when we meet again!

Actually, Canon Holland says we hover between two different responses to death. The one in the passage above, and this other one. Why do you think this is not used at funerals?

> **2** [Death embodies] the supreme and irrevocable disaster. It is the impossible, the incredible thing. Nothing leads up to it, nothing prepares for it. It makes all we do here meaningless and empty. 'Vanity, vanity, all is vanity.' Everything goes to one place, good and bad, just and unjust, happy and unhappy, rich and poor, all lie down together in one common ruin. All are cut off by the same blind inexorable fate. So stated it is inexplicable, so ruthless, so blundering – this death that we must die. It is the cruel ambush into which we are snared. It is the pit of destruction. It wrecks, it defeats, it shatters. Its methods are so cruelly accidental, so wickedly fantastic and freakish. We can never tell when or how its blow will fall.
> It may be, no doubt, that it may come to the very old as the fitting close of an honourable life. But how often it smites, without discrimination, as if it had no law! It makes its horrible breach in our gladness with careless and inhuman disregard of us. There is no light or hope in the grave. Its shadow falls across our natural sunlight, and we are swept off into some black abyss.

Canon Holland believes in a combination of these two views. Would this offer comfort?

> **3** The contrasted experiences are equally real, equally valid. They can only be reconciled through the idea of growth. We are in a condition of process, of growth, of which our state on earth is but the preliminary condition. So, in one sense we know all that lies before us [it is like being in the next room], and in another sense we know nothing of it [it is the abyss].
> We are now the sons of God, which means that now we are already what we will be in the afterlife. 'For you have died and your life is hidden with Christ in God. ['When Christ, who is your life, appears, then you also will appear with him in glory.' Colossians 3:3-4] From this point of view, death is but an accident. We shall simply go on being what we already are. Death does not count.
> And yet ... we can see nothing ahead. How can we picture it? Death shuts fast the door. Beyond that darkness hides its impenetrable secret. We only know that our living experience, the warmth of present companionship, will be gone. Ah! Woe, woe!
> But ... we are already in Jesus. We have Jesus now, and even now we can make ourselves ready to draw closer to Him. ... Have we not the gift of the Spirit? And the Spirit we now possess is itself the Life of all Life, the Life of the Life beyond death. ... In the power of the Spirit we are already passed from death to life. We have the Spirit of Him who says: 'I am the Resurrection and the Life. The one who believes in Me will live, even though they die; and whoever lives by believing in me will never die.' [John 11:25-26]

How do people's beliefs about life after death affect how they live?

Overview

This section of the book explores how our beliefs about life after death make an impact. If you believe that when we die we may go to heaven, or be reincarnated, or rot in a coffin, then what difference does it make? Points of view from Hinduism, Christianity and atheism are used to stimulate students' own thinking. The main learning activity is a multi-path narrative, in which the questions of the impact of belief are explored through making the student a character in a story. The second learning activity uses a 'silent argument' (conducted on paper) to explore reasons why people hold such different views, particularly focusing on argumentative and reasoning skills. The final resource encourages students to reflect on how beliefs can change a person's perspective on life and death.

Essential knowledge

From this work, students will gain an understanding of some key ideas about the human soul, heaven, reincarnation and about the ways in which beliefs have an impact on life in different religions and worldviews.

They will learn that various different viewpoints on ultimate questions about life's purposes and destiny can be defended with reasons in different ways.

They will be challenged to develop good, thoughtful reasons for the views and ideas which they hold themselves.

Essential teaching and learning

This section gives a dramatic twist to thinking about life after death, using a multi-path narrative, a story in which the choices the reader makes lead on to the next part of the story. This 'hook' is developed so that students use the terminology of the debate and are offered chances to evaluate reasons and arguments.

The narrative is written here for class use, led by a teacher, with some writing for students at different points. It is also easily possible to use the narrative for discussion in small groups. Many young people taking GCSE or Standard Grade examinations will benefit from the writing practice this gives them, building their skills in being reasonable about religion and belief.

The learning activities are flexible across a range of abilities and ready to use, making for convenient ways to teach.

14–19

Context

Plan to use this work as part of a study of beliefs about life after death and about the ethical impact of beliefs. It connects with GCSE and Standard Grade study of issues of life after death.

Resources/ links

PDFs of pp.28 and 29 are is available to download from the subscribers'/members area on the RE Today website.

A slide show supporting the activities in this article is also available.

Learning activities

1 Multi-path narrative

The work needs a little preparation, and runs in eight small 'chunks'.

Tell the students they will become a character in a narrative, and will face various choices. They will need to write down their choices and ideas. A piece of A4 paper split into four on each side is a good framework for this.

1. Teach from pp.26-7. Read section 1, 'Disaster'. Ask students to write their thoughts in three minutes.

2. For section 2, ask who would choose the Hindu, the Christian or the atheist chaplain, and read each section aloud. Students write their thoughts about what their chosen chaplain says.

3. Read out section 3, 'A life-changing experience!' Ask pupils to form three groups according to which answer they choose, and discuss briefly within the group how the conversation might unfold. Give them five minutes to write the next few lines of a dialogue.

4. Read sections 4A–4C aloud to the groups who choose them, or get them to read for each other. They do the writing tasks.

5. Read section 5 of the scenario, 'The aftermath'. What choices do they think are possible?

6. Get students to pair and discuss with someone who makes the same choice as them at section 6, then ask them to write their response quietly. This one may need about five minutes, but keep the writing bursts short and sharp.

7. Read section 7. Each student writes their thoughts.

8. Again, divide the class into three as they choose between options 8A, 8B and 8C. There is a writing and thinking task for each student. The scenario can, of course, be extended by the students: you could go back to visit the chaplains/ share your new ideas about life with your (unsupportive) parents/ describe what happens six months later in Hindu India, Roman Catholic Brazil or Muslim Indonesia/ another direction.

2 Impact, impact, impact

Emphasise to your students that whatever we believe, it usually makes a difference. Trace, through the story, the impact of experiences and beliefs on the protagonists.

3 Follow-up

A good homework task is to ask students to write a 'chapter two' for the narrative: what might happen next? Make sure they use the following words: heaven/moksha/ judgement/amazing/evidence/belief/sceptical/open-minded.

4 Six argumentative snippets

On p.28 you will find a further task which aims to enable students to develop argumentative skills. There are many different ways you can use this, including the strategy called 'silent argument', which works through written comments and passing sheets from group to group. It is described at the bottom of p.28, so that students can understand it, and you can adapt as suits your context.

5 Discuss, write, create

Page 29 may be copied for student use or downloaded and printed from the RE Today website by members. It is probably worth making colour copies, one between two. The activity is best tackled after the other work, to bring out the focus on the impact of beliefs about life before death, and after death.

Outcomes

Students can demonstrate achievement at levels 6–8 in these activities (equivalent to GCSE grades C–A) if they can say 'yes' to some of these 'I can' statements.

Description of achievement

I can …

Level 6

- express insights into some ways that beliefs about life after death have an impact on people's behaviour

- interpret a range of different ideas about life after death, giving reasoned arguments to support my own ideas.

Level 7

- give coherent accounts of three different views about life after death, and the arguments and evidence that are used to support these ideas

- use a range of sources and arguments to synthesise my responses to complex questions about life after death.

Level 8

- use a range of different disciplines (e.g. psychology of religion, philosophy, theology) to analyse ideas about life after death

- draw balanced conclusions about why different people hold different beliefs about life after death and its relevance to 'life before death'.

This unit helps students in Scotland to achieve RME 3-09c, 4-09e.

A multi-path narrative to explore ideas about hope, life and death

1 Disaster

So there you are, aged 23. You have been in a dreadful car crash, with your new partner. Your relationship has been great, but now this: you find yourselves in adjacent beds, on a drip, bandaged up. You watch your lovely partner, still unconscious in the bed next to you. S/he seems even worse off than you. You wonder if both of you are dying.

For the first time in your life you consider in a rather personal way the questions:

Is there life after death? And what form does it take? And is there judgement? Heaven? Hell? Oblivion? God? Bliss? Pain? Nothing? What?

You think back over your religious beliefs and spiritual ideas of life, death and beyond, and wish you had paid more attention in RE at school! What is it that Hindus teach? And atheists? And Christians? You decide to ask to speak to one of the hospital chaplains. Do you call for the Hindu chaplain, the Christian, or the atheist?

Write down your thoughts.

2A Hindu

The chaplain comes along and sits with you. He is very calm and seems wise. You ask what the Hindu teaching is about life after death. 'It's like this,' he says. 'When your clothes are worn out, then you have new ones. When your physical body is worn out, then the true self, the "you inside" goes from this life into another body, like a new set of clothes, and your life goes on. You are reincarnated. The good deeds you have done in the last 23 years will help you in the next life, even if you die today. But ...' he smiles, 'I hope you live, though, and your partner.'

Write down your thoughts.

2B Christian

The chaplain comes to chat with you. She is friendly and seems to empathise with you. She says how sorry she is about your accident. You ask: what do Christians think happens when we die? You eye your partner in the next bed. 'Well,' the chaplain replies, 'we believe that there is one true God full of love, your creator. We believe that everyone who trusts God can be received into heaven when we die. It's a place or a state we don't know much about, but it is where human life is fulfilled and all happiness is completed. But would you like me to pray for you both to get well?'

Write down your thoughts.

2C Atheist

When the atheist chaplain comes to see you, he seems likable and thoughtful. You say, 'You don't believe in heaven, do you?' He smiles a bit ruefully. 'No. But I do try to be realistic and compassionate,' he says. 'When we think of the end of life, it can only make us sad, but it is important to make the most of every day, every hour. I do hope you and your partner will have time together, and the medical staff will be effective and save your lives. In the meantime, I'll be here for you. How can I be helpful?'

Write down your thoughts.

3 A life-changing experience!

Questions zoom through your mind, and you decide to ask one. Write down your question.

The chaplain answers your question, giving you plenty to think about. You lie in the bed, drifting in and out of consciousness. Then, suddenly, your partner in the next bed speaks. You are delighted – you had been so scared.

S/he says: 'This is incredible! Are you OK? I feel terrible, but I've just had the most extraordinary dream! It was as if I had died, and experienced the whole of life in a flash. It was really strange. You know me, I don't believe in any weird stuff, but I felt this amazing sense of being at one with – well – everything. I felt totally confident that everything will be all right. I could see this blinding light. But then it all faded away, and I'm back here. What sense can you make of that?' S/he looks suddenly terrified: 'Are we dying?' s/he asks.

What do you say next?

  A 'The chaplains all seem good. Do you want to talk to one of them?'
  B 'I think you must be going a little crazy with the pain. Shall I get the nurse to give you something for it?'
  C 'Wow! That is amazing! Do you really think there could be a life beyond this life?'

Write down your conversation.

4A Chaplains

The Hindu chaplain says 'This could be a kind of premonition of the next life.' The Christian chaplain says 'This could be an important experience, and you should explore it.' The atheist, gently, says 'Don't make too much of this, it's probably just a dream, a bit of delirium.'

Who do you agree with, and why?

Write your answer.

4B Discussion

S/he replies: 'Well, I didn't believe before, but it feels to me as if I have just been halfway there. I think there must be something after death. Maybe your soul takes a journey to get there. What do you think?'

You open your mouth, but are not sure what to say.

Write down how you would reply.

4C Pain relief

You call the nurse and she brings more pain relief for your partner. But into your head comes this idea: 'I don't think it is good just to dismiss this question as crazy. What if s/he really did "half die" and come back?' You make a mental list of points for and against this possibility.

Make the lists of points 'for and against'.

5 The aftermath

You are a bit amazed by all that seems to be going on. You write all about it in your diary.

The next morning, you are so relieved when you wake up to see your partner sitting up, awake, looking a little better, drinking water. You ask how s/he is feeling. 'Unbelievable,' s/he says. 'Way better than before the accident, because for the first time in my life I feel like I'm sure there is life after death. So what are we going to do about that?'

Do you ask the chaplains for ideas again, or discuss it with your partner?

6A

You agree to ask the chaplains how beliefs about life after death make a difference. Each one gives an interesting answer that makes you think:

'**Hindus** always seek to build up good karma, so that our cycle of birth and death is onwards and upwards.'

'**Christians** hope for heaven so we try to follow Jesus and live lives full of faith and generosity.'

'**Atheists** are pretty sure that this life is all we have, so we're determined to enjoy it, and make it better for others.'

Write down the next question you decide to ask each of the chaplains. How do you think they would reply?

6B

You discuss your partner's vision. S/he says 'I just think it is amazing to know that there is something after this life. We need to change our lives. We should go round the world and see what all the religions say. We need to give up our jobs and give our money to the poor. Wow, it's amazing!'

You are not so sure. Do you:

• ask for more details about her/his ideas?
• reply saying you will not be doing this, and you might break up?
• reply saying that it sounds like a great idea and start discussing plans?

Write down the conversation you have.

7 Three months on

You and your partner have recovered and are both out of hospital, fit and well. The conversation about life after death goes on. S/he says that what we believe has to make a difference. You get this point, but you are not agreed about what difference it should make. S/he wants to give up work, give away a lot of money, and travel in search of the answers to her/his questions, saying 'Now I know for sure there is life after death, it seems less important to focus on careers and money.'

Which parts of these views do you find hardest? Which do you agree with most? **Write your thoughts.**

8A Travelling in search of wise answers

You both agree that travel would be good, and make a plan. Where would you go and who would you try to meet if you wanted to answer this question: what difference does belief about the next life make to this life?

Plan your trip.

8B Letting this world go and focusing on the next world

You both agree that whether heaven or reincarnation are the reality, you want to stop chasing money and promotion and start living for others. You discuss three ways to change your lives.

Write down the three ways, and the reasons why you are going to make these changes.

8C Living one life well

You both agree that this life is all we have, so you want to live it well. You discuss what this means, and come up with three ways to change your lives after your experiences of coming close to death.

Write down the three ways, and the reasons why you are going to make these changes.

6 Reasoned beliefs about the afterlife: a silent argument strategy

I believe that when we are dead, that is the end of us. The different religions all disagree (heaven or reincarnation? Those are not the same at all.).
I don't say they are stupid, just that there is no real evidence for any form of survival of the 'soul'.
Like a dead plant or animal, a human's consciousness stops when the body dies. So for me, all ideas about heaven, hell, angels, paradise, meeting God and being judged are highly improbable.

'If only someone could come back from the grave and tell us what really happens ...' Lots of agnostics say this. Well, two billion Christians believe this is exactly what did happen! Jesus, God on earth, died and was buried. After three days he was resurrected, and over six weeks showed his followers what the next life is like. I believe in life after death because Jesus was the prototype. When we die, our true personality – say 'soul' if you like – does not finish with death. It is resurrected, like Jesus!

Imagine for a moment that there is life after death in some form – your consciousness survives somehow. Imagine the rumours of ghosts and spiritualism, mediums and messages from the dead actually tell us something vague but true. If this was reality, then surely it would not be so easy to fake (thanks, Derren Brown). And above that, surely some sense would come back from beyond the grave, instead of all the vague 'does someone here today have a reason to be sad?' It's all nonsense!

The average human body contains enough iron to make a three-inch nail. Enough sulphur to kill the fleas on a dog. Enough carbon to make 900 pencils. Enough potassium to fire a toy cannon. Enough fat for 7 bars of soap. Enough phosphorous to make 2200 matches. The rest is pretty much all water, about 45 litres. It's the same stuff in your body, whether you are dead or alive. But the main thing, the 'you', the personality, has gone. Do you really believe you are nothing more than the list above? The 'you' who laughs and loves, plays, sings, feels passion and sorrow, is the real you. And might survive ...

I am arguing that the soul is not real. Religions all seem to agree that 'soul' (or 'atman' as Hindus call it) is a thing. But the brain is a physical part of the human body, and the electrical activity between neurones is observable. The soul is not observable – no microscope or MRI scanner can detect any such thing.
So, simply: no soul, no life after death.

I've got a moral argument for life after death. It goes like this. There are great injustices in the world. Life is unfair. In any one generation, many good people suffer and some evil people prosper. If God (the Universe? Brahman?) is just, then only in a life beyond this life can injustice be put right. Hindus (believing in karma) and Christians (believing in heavenly rewards) both teach that the justice of God/ the Ultimate is not fully shown in this life. It is in the next life that justice will be balanced. You can reject this – but if you do, you also reject the idea of justice. That's a high price to pay.

Learning activities

- Position each quotation in the centre of a large sheet of paper.
- Read one quotation aloud in a group of four. Then, in silence, write down your reactions to this quote – questions it raises, reasons to agree, reasons to disagree.
- Pass the annotated sheet on to the next group. Take a new sheet from another group, and read out the quotation. Add comments, reactions, questions and points about the quotation or other students' comments. Pass it on again.
- At the third 'pass' you can only write criticisms or alternative arguments to previous comments. Carry on the silent argument.
- Display the filled-in sheets on the wall. Look together at how ideas have developed. Underline or circle the best points you have read.

Is life mainly hope and happiness or darkness and despair?

hanks to Mia Payne, 13, from William Allitt School, Derbyshire. Image © NATRE

Mia is 13. Here she reflects on her ideas and beliefs about life's light and dark experiences.

'I have drawn the silhouette of a woman's face, showing just one eye and her lips. You may think you know what's going on in life, but you can't see everything. Things happen without your consent: you have to deal with the things that happen in life. Friends will deceive you, family will lie to you and you won't always know when or why! This may lead to sad times in your life, represented by the dark, dull colours of the woman's hair, but not all is bad, as shown by the bright rainbow colours of the woman's face.

'I have made my drawing so that miserably dark hair surrounds the bright happiness of the face. When there is a happy time in your life, if you are enjoying life at the moment, there will eventually be a downside. Something will make the happiness fade and seem like it was too good to be true. However, this also applies for the darker parts of life; there will always be a moment where it all seems worth it.'

Discuss, write, create

What does Mia believe? Why? How can you tell?

The Christian Bible says: 'Do not be anxious about anything, but in everything, by praying and asking God, make your requests known to God. And then the peace of God, which is beyond our understanding, will keep your hearts and minds safe in Christ.' (Paul in Philippians 4:6-7). How might Mia's view of life and death change if she agreed with this?

The Hindu scriptures say: 'Brahman (the ultimate reality) shines out. Vast, self-luminous, inconceivable, subtler than the subtle. He is far beyond what is far, and yet here very near at hand. He is seen here, living in the cave of the heart of every conscious being' (*Mundaka Upanishad*). What does the scripture mean? Try putting it into simple language, say for eight-year-olds! How might Mia's view of life and death change if she agreed with this?

What do you say? Express your own beliefs. You could do this in art, like Mia, or in poetry, or in writing a creed. Make sure you think about, and express the impact of your beliefs: what difference do your beliefs make, compared to other beliefs? Tentative ideas are fine, but do explain why you are not quite sure.

Topical
artefact: Crazy Coffins

A coffin by Paa Joe: for a former deep sea fisherman

For the former owner of a fleet of cars (Paa Joe)

A 16-year-old boy died. His mother ordered a replica of his E71 Nokia mobile phone as his coffin, built to dimensions suitable for cremation.

The egg shape was commissioned for a woman who wanted to be cremated in the foetal position. The egg is a symbol of birth and new life, so is perhaps a fitting symbol of a hope for life after death.

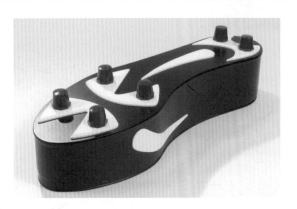

A design on offer for the committed fan.

The deceased had always desired a yacht during his lifetime.

Learning activities

Joseph Ashong, or Paa Joe as he is known, is a coffin-maker from Ghana, West Africa. He is one of a number of such coffin designers/makers in the country. His elaborate coffins are designed to represent something important to the person being buried.

This idea has spread further afield, with UK coffin makers such as Crazy Coffins in Nottingham creating a bespoke service.

NB. Bear in mind that looking at coffins may be distressing for some students.

Some questions to get you started

What are the advantages of buying now and dying later?

Why would someone want a coffin like this?

Are they too frivolous for a solemn moment – or does it reflect the absurdity of life and death? Or should funerals be times of celebration, not gloom?

For whose benefit are these coffins made – the dead or the living?

How does it compare to ancient rituals of burying warriors or kings with the accoutrements of their lives, in order to furnish them with what they need for an afterlife?

Or does this fashion reflect contemporary obsession with the material goods of this world? Do they indicate a hope for a future life, or a clinging to this material existence?

What would Jesus, Guru Nanak or the Buddha say?

Many places offer cardboard, reed or even woollen coffins. Why do people want these more 'natural' funerals?

Is burial within a wood an attractive idea, serving to enrich the soil for plant life? Is this more than just environmentally prudent – does it serve as a metaphor for a form of afterlife?

Some activities to try out

There is fun to be had in looking at these coffins and considering what designs might appeal to different people. However, spending time designing their own would be macabre and inappropriate, and more to do with Design Technology than RE. So …

1 Look at a selection of coffins. What do they reveal about what matters most to the person, and how?

2 Ask students to consider whether these are seriously important or actually trivial:
   a if this life is all there is
   b if there is some form of life after death.

   Discuss who is more likely to have one of these 'crazy coffin' designs – a Christian or an atheist? Why?

3 If there is an afterlife, everyone agrees that you cannot take anything with you when you die. This means that something of your character or personality – something that is the essential 'you' – is what matters. Decide what top three essential qualities might fit someone for eternal life (e.g. love, confidence, compassion, creativity?). How might a coffin design express these qualities/virtues/gifts?

Links/resources

More images from Paa Joe available: http://www.jackbellgallery.com/artists/35-Paa-Joe/overview/

More information about Paa Joe and the Ghanaian coffin workshop: http://www.independent.co.ug/society/society/5127-paa-joe-the-ghanan-coffin-maker

Visit Crazy Coffins at www.crazycoffins.co.uk

See their top ten coffin designs here: http://www.bbc.co.uk/nottingham/content/image_galleries/crazy_coffins_gallery.shtml

Hear about the work of the coffin designer and see some of their remarkable coffin creations: http://www.youtube.com/watch?v=2B0W-ZA6jAI

Natural coffins: http://www.naturalendings.co.uk/our-coffins/

Entry-level activities

Euphemisms

In an age where we do not often encounter death directly, we tend to talk about it indirectly. We talk about people passing on, or passing away. Euphemisms such as these disguise what is an uncomfortable reality with pleasant-sounding alternatives. They are nice ways of saying something nasty, although some of the terms below are not so pleasant.

1 Give your students this selection of terms for death and ask them to add their own.
2 Can they sort them into any categories? What are they? An obvious pair of categories is that some suggest this life is all there is, whereas others hint at some kind of continuation or new life.
3 Talk about the differences, and why we speak in this way about death and dying.
4 What are the advantages or disadvantages of using euphemisms?
5 Use the cover art to identify which of these euphemisms are illustrated. Perhaps students might like to produce artworks in the style of Si Smith for the remaining terms?

Passed away	Food for worms
Gone to sleep	Gone to meet her Maker
Dead as a doornail	Gone to the other side
Six feet under	Snuffed it
Gone to the great golf course/ football stadium/? in the sky	In Paradise
Gone to a better place	Kicked the bucket
With the angels	Popped his clogs
At rest	Fitted with a wooden overcoat
Croaked	With Jesus
Facing Judgment	In Davy Jones' locker